Mysterious Disappearances

Kevin Walker

Rourke
Educational Media

rourkeeducationalmedia.com

Before, During, and After Reading Activities

Before Reading: Building Background Knowledge and Academic Vocabulary

"Before Reading" strategies activate prior knowledge and set a purpose for reading. Before reading a book, it is important to tap into what your child or students already know about the topic. This will help them develop their vocabulary and increase their reading comprehension.

Questions and activities to build background knowledge:
1. *Look at the cover of the book. What will this book be about?*
2. *What do you already know about the topic?*
3. *Let's study the Table of Contents. What will you learn about in the book's chapters?*
4. *What would you like to learn about this topic? Do you think you might learn about it from this book? Why or why not?*

Building Academic Vocabulary

Building academic vocabulary is critical to understanding subject content.
Assist your child or students to gain meaning of the following vocabulary words.

Content Area Vocabulary

Read the list. What do these words mean?

- adrift
- alias
- artifacts
- civilization
- colony
- tropical

During Reading: Writing Component

"During Reading" strategies help to make connections, monitor understanding, generate questions, and stay focused.
1. *While reading, write in your reading journal any questions you have or anything you do not understand.*
2. *After completing each chapter, write a summary of the chapter in your reading journal.*
3. *While reading, make connections with the text and write them in your reading journal.*
   a) *Text to Self – What does this remind me of in my life? What were my feelings when I read this?*
   b) *Text to Text – What does this remind me of in another book I've read? How is this different from other books I've read?*
   c) *Text to World – What does this remind me of in the real world? Have I heard about this before? (News, current events, school, etc.…)*

After Reading: Comprehension and Extension Activity

"After Reading" strategies provide an opportunity to summarize, question, reflect, discuss, and respond to text. After reading the book, work on the following questions with your child or students to check their level of reading comprehension and content mastery.
1. What is a ghost ship? *(Summarize)*
2. Why has the Bermuda Triangle become so famous? *(Infer)*
3. What was Amelia Earhart doing when she disappeared? *(Asking Questions)*
4. Which mysterious disappearance is the most interesting to you and why? *(Text to Self Connection)*

Extension Activity

Think about two or three of the mysterious disappearances mentioned in this book. Write your own explanation for what you think really happened. Discuss why your explanation makes the most sense.

Table of Contents

Lost at Sea

In 1872, the *Mary Celeste* was found **adrift**. The crew had vanished.

WHERE DID THEY GO?

Pirates may have kidnapped the crew. Some people think a waterspout swept them off the ship.

adrift (uh-DRIFT): drifting or floating freely through water or air

In 1931, the SS *Baychimo* got trapped in Arctic ice. The crew built a hut nearby to wait for a thaw. When they awoke one morning, the ship was gone!

COLD CASE

The crew thought the ship sank. But people saw this "Ghost Ship of the Arctic" floating in the frozen seas many times for the next 40 years.

Into Thin Air

Amelia Earhart set out to fly around the world in 1937. She never made it back. Most people think she crashed in the Pacific Ocean. But no one has ever found her remains or the wreckage.

WILD THEORIES

Some conspiracy theories claim Amelia landed and was captured by the Japanese. Others think she was a spy who got caught.

Amelia Earhart was the first woman to fly nonstop and solo across the Atlantic Ocean.

A man using the **alias** D.B. Cooper held a plane hostage in 1971. He demanded money and parachutes. Then he jumped out of the plane into a thunderstorm!

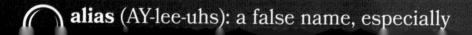

alias (AY-lee-uhs): a false name, especially

The mysterious man was never found. No one knows who or where he is, nor what he did with the money.

Some people just simply vanish. Ambrose Bierce, a famous writer, told his family he was joining the Mexican Revolution. No one heard from him again.

"Speak when you are angry and you will make the best speech you will ever regret."

— *Ambrose Bierce*

The Bermuda Triangle is the site of many
mysterious ship and airplane disappearances.
In 1945, five bomber planes disappeared.
Another plane disappeared during the search.

POSSIBLE EXPLANATIONS

Dozens of ships and planes have disappeared in the Bermuda Triangle. Some people think magnetic waves cause planes and ships to get lost, then crash or sink.

Lost People, Lost Places

Roanoke
Island

A United States **colony** disappeared without a trace. In 1587, 120 English colonists settled on Roanoke Island off the coast of North Carolina.

By 1590, all had vanished. The only clue was the name of a nearby island and American Indian tribe, Croatoan, carved into a tree.

colony (KAH-luh-nee): a group of people who leave their country to settle in a new area

When it comes to disappearances, perhaps the biggest mystery is the lost **civilization** of Atlantis. Some think it was destroyed in a volcano eruption, if it really existed at all.

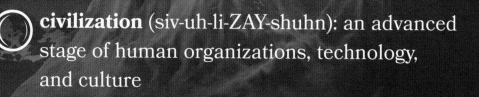

civilization (siv-uh-li-ZAY-shuhn): an advanced stage of human organizations, technology, and culture

PLATO'S STORY

Greek philosopher Plato first mentioned Atlantis in one of his books. He wrote that the island nation angered the Greek gods and was sunk in the Atlantic Ocean.

Percy Harrison Fawcett was a great adventurer. He often searched for **artifacts** and lost civilizations. In 1925, Percy vanished in the Amazon jungle while looking for a lost city he called "Z."

artifacts (AHR-tuh-fakts): objects made or changed by human beings, especially a tool or weapon used in the past

INDY INSPIRATION

Percy Harrison Fawcett may have served as the inspiration for movie adventurer Indiana Jones.

Mu, sometimes called Lemuria, was said to be a **tropical** paradise before the island sank somewhere in the Pacific thousands of years ago.

tropical (TRAH-pi-kuhl): having to do with the hot, rainy area of the tropics

The Mayan people lived for centuries in Mexico. But more than a thousand years ago, they abandoned their great cities. Archeologists have mapped thousands of Mayan structures hidden deep in the jungle.

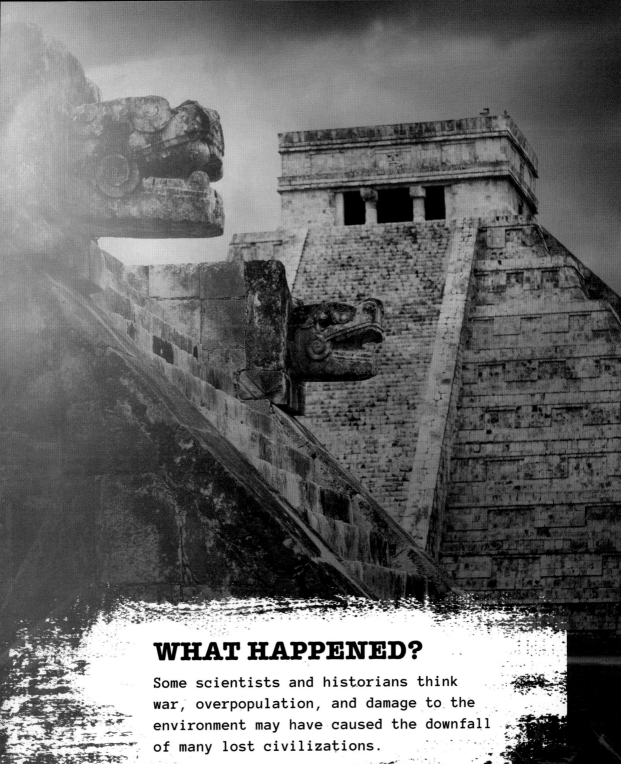

WHAT HAPPENED?

Some scientists and historians think war, overpopulation, and damage to the environment may have caused the downfall of many lost civilizations.

The great city of Thonis, Egypt, sat at the mouth of the Nile River. It sank into the Mediterranean Sea more than a thousand years ago. Scientists think it may have been destroyed by an earthquake.

FRANCE

ATLANTIC OCEAN

Sea of Azov

SLOVENIA
CROATIA

Ligurian Sea

Gulf of Lion

ITALY

Adriatic Sea

Black Sea

Bosphorus

Corsica

Tyrrhenian Sea

Strait of Otranto

ALBANIA

Sea of Marmara

Thracian Sea

SPAIN

Balearic Sea

Balearic Islands

Sardinia

MEDITERRANEAN

GREECE

Aegean Sea

Dardanelles

TURKEY

PORTUGAL

Sicily

Ionian Sea

Myrtoan Sea

Gulf of Antalya

Strait of Gibraltar

Alboran Sea

Sea of Sicily

Strait of Messina

SEA

Sea of Crete

Cyprus

SYRIA

MALTA

Crete

Levantine Sea

LEBANON

ALGERIA

Gulf of Gabes

Libyan Sea

ISRAEL

MOROCCO

TUNISIA

Thonis
☆

Gulf of Sidra

LIBYA

EGYPT

Nile River ☆

27

**Easter
Island**

Easter Island was home to a great civilization. They built famous stone statues that still stand.

But they also chopped down trees and used up farmland. Many experts think they disappeared because they ran out of food!

Memory Game

Can you match the image to what you read?

Index

Show What You Know

1. Who first mentioned Atlantis?

2. Where did the Mayan people live?

3. Where is the Bermuda Triangle located?

4. What was Percy Harrison Fawcett looking for when he disappeared?

5. Who was Ambrose Bierce?

Further Reading

Jazynka, Kitson, *History's Mysteries: Freaky Phenomenon: Curious Clues, Cold Cases, and Puzzles from the Past*, National Geographic Children's Books, 2018.

MacLeod, Elizabeth, *Vanished: True Tales of Mysterious Disappearances*, Annick Press, 2016.

Stilton, Thea, *The Journey to Atlantis*, Scholastic Paperbacks, 2012.

About the Author

Kevin Walker is a writer and journalist who hopes to never mysteriously disappear.

Meet The Author!
www.meetREMauthors.com

www.rourkeeducationalmedia.com

PHOTO CREDITS: Cover and Title Pg ©Wiki, ©Olga_Z; Pg 4 - 32 ©FOTOKITA; Pg 5, 10, 17, 18, 20, 23 ©marlanu; Pg 3 ©FOTOKITA, ©Grafissimo; Pg 4 ©Placebo365; Pg 4 & 30 ©Wiki; Pg 5 ©Gannet77; Pg 6 ©Allexxandar; Pg 7 ©Aldus Books London; Pg 8 ©igs942, ©holwichaikawee; Pg 9 ©Wiki; Pg 10 ©Sjo, ©Mauricio Graiki; Pg 11 ©GordZam, ©greenaperture; Pg 12 ©Library of Congress, ©Allexxandar; Pg 13 & 30 ©Wiki; Pg 14 & 30 ©Lightguard; Pg 15 ©lindsay_imagery, ©Wiki; Pg 16 ©Wiki; Pg 17 ©Wiki; Pg 18 ©solarseven; Pg 19 ©RaphaelQS; Pg 20 ©Mlenny; Pg 21 & 30 ©Ginomad wiki; Pg 22 ©IakovKalinin; Pg 23 ©ftwitty; Pg 24 ©Orbon Alija, Pg 24 & 30 ©EugeneTomeev; Pg 25 ©YinYang; Pg 26 ©usas, ©seyfettinozel; Pg 27 ©opulent-images, ©Wiki; Pg 28 ©xingmin07; Pg 29 & 30 ©Mlenny

Edited by: Keli Sipperley
Cover and interior design by: Kathy Walsh

Library of Congress PCN Data

Mysterious Disappearances / Kevin Walker
  (Unexplained)
  ISBN 978-1-64369-034-6 (hard cover)
  ISBN 978-1-64369-104-6 (soft cover)
  ISBN 978-1-64369-181-7 (e-Book)
Library of Congress Control Number: 2018956019

Rourke Educational Media
Printed in the United States of America,
North Mankato, Minnesota

3 1333 04895 5593